Messianic Family Haggadah

Arranged by Janie-sue Wertheim

Messianic Family Haggadah
Arranged by Janie-sue Wertheim

© 2007 by Purple Pomegranate Productions
(a division of Jews for Jesus®)
Edited by Susan Perlman
Cover painting by Nina Freifeld-Giles
Inside drawings by David Blankenship and David Yapp
Design by David Yapp

All rights reserved. Nothing in this book shall be reprinted or reproduced, electronically or in any other manner, without express written permission.

For more information, including reprint permission, write to:
Jews for Jesus®
60 Haight Street
San Francisco, CA 94102
USA
www.jewsforjesus.org

ISBN 10: 1 881022 80 3
ISBN 13: 978 1 881022 80 0

ACKNOWLEDGMENTS

Special thanks to the children of our camp ministry, Camp Gilgal, who spurred me on to put together an earlier draft of a family friendly haggadah for their use. This final product began in the hearts of our young campers and their parents who wanted to rejoice in the rich heritage we have as Jewish believers in Jesus. To my friend Kathy Shapiro, who spurred this project on by testing a version of this haggadah with her own family. To Nina Freifeld-Giles, who sat at Kathy's Passover table and was so inspired that she donated her beautiful original artwork for the cover illustration. Thanks to Melissa Moskowitz for her substantial contribution to the recipes section; to David Blankenship and David Yapp for their artistic embellishments throughout the haggadah; to Stephen Katz, for the helpful comments he gave on Passover traditions; and to Rich Robinson who worked with Stephen on the Hebrew and transliteration. Thanks also to Susan Perlman for her editing skills and encouragement throughout this project.

A word of thanks as well to the authors of the haggadot we have published that preceded this one—the work of the late Eric Lipson who provided a wealth of Jewish insights and Messianic jewels in *Passover Haggadah* and the work of Joan Lipis whose volume *Celebrate Passover Haggadah* opened the eyes of Gentile believers to include Passover in their home celebrations.

PREFACE

The *Messianic Family Haggadah* has been planned with families in mind. Explanations are given so that both children and adults can take part with understanding. Illustrations are child-friendly. Instructions are written out so that even the novice Passover leader can confidently officiate at a family seder. The service is intended to be both edifying and fun.

Passover services can be lengthy, somewhat brief or anywhere in between. You will have much liberty to condense or expand depending on your personal taste and the attention span of your children. If we have erred in the content, we hope it is in giving you more to choose from rather than less. Feel free to cut out what might be too lengthy for your family to handle. It is "traditional" in Jewish homes to do this, so don't feel guilty! And don't feel guilty if your haggadot inherit some food stains over the years—that's part of our families' traditions too.

While this Messianic Haggadah keeps the essential elements of the traditional seder service, Bible passages from the New Testament as well as the Hebrew Scriptures are woven throughout its pages. The link is made between the Exodus event that marks the first Passover and the Calvary event which takes this Festival of Redemption to its deeper meaning.

If you are a Jewish believer in Jesus (Y'shua), this service has been prepared especially for you. As part of the appendices, you'll notice we have included some traditional Passover recipes that might even rival your *bubbe's* (grandmother's) culinary delights. We've also included the traditional Passover songs you have been singing since you were a child as well as some Messianic Passover songs that can become "new" traditions to pass on to your children. And if you are a little rusty on your Hebrew, we've also included transliterated versions of the traditional prayers and songs found throughout the Haggadah.

If you are a kosher-hearted Gentile believer in Jesus who has a desire to get in on this rich family celebration, this Haggadah is for you too! It will provide a satisfying experience for you and your children and an opportunity to appreciate the Jewish roots of your faith.

The *Messianic Family Haggadah* is for believers of all ages and traditions who want to give honor and glory to Jesus, our Passover Lamb and Redeemer. So enjoy!

—Janie-sue Wertheim

PREPARATION FOR THE PASSOVER

The following items are needed to set your Passover table:

1. Wine cup at each place setting and enough Passover wine or grape juice to fill the cup four times
2. Matzah (enough so that everyone at the table can have at least one board). Three pieces of *matzah* should be wrapped in either a traditional *matzah tash* or in between three pieces of white linen and placed by the leader of the seder.
3. Seder Plate, which holds the following items:
   a. *Karpas*: Use either a bunch of parsley, celery or lettuce
   b. *Chazeret*: Horseradish root or whole onion (do not peel)
   c. *Maror*: Ground horseradish in a small bowl
   d. *Beitzah*: Roasted or hard boiled egg
   e. *Charoset*: Apple and nut mixture (see recipes on page 78)
   f. *Z'roa*: shankbone of a lamb
   g. Bowl of salt water (use more than one for easy access by everyone at the table)
4. Basin of water and towel
5. Two candlesticks, candles and matches
6. Cup of Elijah (large goblet filled with wine and put near the center of the table)
7. Pillow or cushion to put on the left side of the leader's seat
8. Optional items: traditional white *kittel* (robe) and *mitre* (cantor's cap) for the head of the household, and *kippot* or *yarmulkes* (skullcaps) for each male participant

KEY

The following roles are to be set and a person designated to fulfill them before the seder begins:

Leader

Woman of the house

Reader 1

Reader 2

Child to recite the Four Questions

When it says: "All," everyone at the table is to read.

GUIDE TO PRONUNCIATION

Some vowels can be pronounced slightly differently depending on the word. When in doubt, use the first of two alternate pronunciations.

"a" as in f**a**ther

"e" as e in b**e**d, sometimes as a in "c**a**ne" (especially in "Eloh**e**nu")

"i" as in p**i**n, sometimes as in k**i**ng

"o" as "oa" in b**oa**t

"u" as in p**u**sh, sometimes as "oo" in m**oo**n

"ai" as "i" in m**i**ne

"ei" as "a" in n**a**me

"ch" as in German a**ch**

"tz" as in ca**ts**

"sh" as in **sh**ip

final h is silent (except "ch" and "sh" as above)

other letters as in English

ORDER OF THE PASSOVER SEDER

1. Lighting of the Candles
2. Blessings Over the Children
3. The First Cup
4. Hand Washing
5. Eating of the Greens
6. Breaking the Middle Matzah
7. The Four Questions
8. The Passover Story
9. The Ten Plagues
10. The Three Symbols of Passover
11. Psalms 113-115
12. The Second Cup
13. Hand Washing Before Meal
14. Special Blessing for the Matzah
15. Eating the Bitter Herbs, *Charoset* and Roasted Egg
16. Serving the Meal
17. Eating the *Afikoman*
18. The Third Cup
19. Grace After the Meal
20. Cup of Elijah
21. Psalms 116-118
22. The Fourth Cup
23. Concluding the Seder
24. Additional Songs

B'DIKAT CHAMETZ   SEARCH FOR THE LEAVEN   בְּדִיקַת חָמֵץ

All: On Passover, the Feast of Unleavened Bread, we are to remember that our ancestors left Egypt in such haste that there was not time for the bread for their journey to rise. And so, we too eat only unleavened bread for the eight days of the holiday. We are not only to refrain from eating all food which contains leaven or *chametz*, but to remove any leaven from our home.

Leader: A special ceremony to memorialize the removal of leaven takes place the night before the first night of Passover (the 13th of Nisan on the Jewish calendar). After the home is thoroughly cleansed of *chametz* by the mother, the father takes a lit candle and with one of his young children at his side, he does a final inspection. First he recites the following prayer:

בָּרוּךְ אַתָּה יְיָ אֱלֹהֵינוּ מֶלֶךְ הָעוֹלָם, אֲשֶׁר קִדְּשָׁנוּ בְּמִצְוֹתָיו וְצִוָּנוּ עַל בִּיעוּר חָמֵץ:

Baruch atah Adonai, Elohenu melech ha-olam, asher kid'shanu b'mitzvotav v'tzivanu al biur chametz.

Blessed are You, O Lord our God, King of the Universe, who has sanctified us by Your commandments and commanded us to remove the leaven.

Reader 1: It is customary to hide a small portion of *chametz* so that something is actually found and the above prayer can be fulfilled. The inspection is then carried out with a feather, a wooden spoon and cloth. Once the leaven is found, the father scoops up the *chametz* and sees to it that all that is found is burned. He then says the following prayer:

כָּל חֲמִירָא וַחֲמִיעָה דְּאִכָּא בִרְשׁוּתִי,
דְּלָא חֲמִיתֵּהּ וּדְלָא בְעַרְתֵּהּ,
לִבָּטֵל וְלֶהֱוֵי הֶפְקֵר, כְּעַפְרָא דְאַרְעָא:

Kol chamira va'chami'ah d'ika virshuti,
D'la chamitei, ud'la viartei,
libatel v'lehevei hefker, k'afra d'ara.

May any manner of leaven that is in my home, which I have not seen or have not removed, be considered as if it does not exist, and as the dust of the earth.

Reader 2: Throughout the Hebrew Scriptures, leaven is symbolic of sin. Our Messiah refers to leaven as false teaching and hypocrisy. A first-century Jew for Jesus, Paul, speaks of leaven as malice and pride. In our preparation for celebrating Passover, let us not only clean our homes of leaven, but use this as an occasion to confess all known sin to God so that we too are cleansed and renewed.

Those assembled, take a moment of silent prayer and confession

THE SEDER BEGINS

Hadlakat ha-Ner   Lighting the Festival Candles   הַדְלָקַת הַנֵר

The woman of the house says the traditional blessing as she lights the candles:

בָּרוּךְ אַתָּה יְיָ אֱלֹהֵינוּ מֶלֶךְ הָעוֹלָם, אֲשֶׁר קִדְּשָׁנוּ בְּמִצְוֹתָיו וְצִוָּנוּ לְהַדְלִיק נֵר שֶׁל יוֹם טוֹב.

Baruch atah Adonai, Elohenu melech ha-olam, asher kid'shanu b'mitzvotav v'tzivanu l'hadlik ner shel yom tov.

Blessed are You, O Lord our God, King of the Universe, who has set us apart by Your commandments and commanded us to light the Festival lights.

Leader: How fitting that it is the mother in the home who brings light to our Passover celebration. For it was through the woman that the One who is Light came into the world.

Reader 1: Messiah Y'shua said of Himself, "I am the light of the world. Whoever follows me will never walk in darkness, but will have the light of life" (John 8:12).

11

Leader: Together, let us all say the Messianic blessing which centers our thoughts on Y'shua.

בָּרוּךְ אַתָּה יְיָ, אֱלֹהֵינוּ מֶלֶךְ הָעוֹלָם, אֲשֶׁר קִדְּשָׁנוּ בְּיֵשׁוּעַ הַמָּשִׁיחַ, אוֹר הָעוֹלָם:

Baruch atah Adonai, Elohenu melech ha-olam, asher kid'shanu b'Y'shua ha-Mashiach, or ha-olam.

Blessed are You, O Lord our God, King of the Universe, who has sanctified us in Y'shua the Messiah, the light of the world.

Wearing of the Kittel

Leader: As the one who presides over this seder, I now put on the *kittel*, the ceremonial robe. It is white, the color of righteousness, the color worn by the high priest and it reminds us of the Temple times. On my head is a white silk *mitre*, (shaped like a crown). This *mitre* symbolizes kingship, and it is said that for the night of Passover, he who presides over the seder is to be king in his home.

BLESSINGS OVER THE CHILDREN PRESENT

Leader: It is traditional in ushering in the Shabbat, that families have a moment where the leader of the home offers a blessing for the male and female children present. At Passover, where children play such a key role in our celebration, it is appropriate to keep this tradition going. *The leader goes around the table and prays for each group of children offering words similar to these:*

For the male children:

Leader: May the Lord make you like Efraim and Manasseh, who received the blessing from their grandfather Jacob and who led lives honoring to God. And may He also make you like Andrew and Peter, the first brothers to leave all behind and follow Y'shua as the promised Messiah. May you trust in God all the days of your life and be ready for Him to use you in great ways even now.

For the female children:

Leader: May the Lord make you like Sarah, Rebekah, Rachel and Leah, who were women of faith who endured hardship, showed courage, loved their husbands and were loyal to God. And may He also make you like Priscilla, an able teacher of the word of God and like Mary and Johanna who ministered to Y'shua. May you trust in God all the days of your life and be ready for Him to use you in great ways even now.

For all the children, the leader then gives the Aaronic Benediction:

יְבָרֶכְךָ יְיָ וְיִשְׁמְרֶךָ:
יָאֵר יְיָ פָּנָיו אֵלֶיךָ וִיחֻנֶּךָ:
יִשָּׂא יְיָ פָּנָיו אֵלֶיךָ וְיָשֵׂם לְךָ שָׁלוֹם:

Y'varech'cha Adonai v'yishm'recha.
Ya'er Adonai panav elecha vi-chuneka.
Yisa Adonai panav elecha v'yasem l'cha shalom.
May the Lord bless you and keep you.

May the Lord bless you and keep you. May He cause His presence to shine on you and be gracious to you. May the Lord turn His face to you and give you wholeness and peace, *in the name of the Prince Peace, Y'shua our shalom.*

KADDESH   CUP OF SANCTIFICATION   קַדֵּשׁ

The first cup is filled and raised.

Leader: The Cup of Sanctification or *Kiddush* is the first of four cups we will drink tonight. *Kiddush* literally means sanctification or imparting holiness. It reminds us that we are set apart for special service to God. As this seder begins, let us remember that as believers in the Messiah we are set apart from that which is of the world, for we belong to Y'shua. As we celebrate *Pesach* let us reflect on the spotless lamb of God who calls us to be holy as He is holy.

Chant the blessing together:

בָּרוּךְ אַתָּה יְיָ, אֱלֹהֵינוּ מֶלֶךְ הָעוֹלָם, בּוֹרֵא פְּרִי הַגָּפֶן:

> Baruch atah Adonai, Elohenu melech ha-olam, borei p'ri ha-gafen.

> Blessed are You, O Lord our God, King of the Universe, who creates the fruit of the vine.

Chant the traditional blessing that marks all seasons and times of rejoicing:

בָּרוּךְ אַתָּה, יְיָ אֱלֹהֵינוּ מֶלֶךְ הָעוֹלָם,
שֶׁהֶחֱיָנוּ וְקִיְּמָנוּ וְהִגִּיעָנוּ לַזְּמַן הַזֶּה:

Baruch atah Adonai, Elohenu melech ha-olam, she-hecheyanu, v'kiy'manu, v'higianu lazman ha-zeh.

Blessed are You, O Lord our God, King of the Universe, who has preserved us in life, established us and enabled us to reach this season.

All: You have provided us O Lord, with seasons for rejoicing, such as this season of Passover, a time to remember the Exodus from Egypt and the redemption of our ancestors out of slavery. You have

chosen us and sanctified us and given us an even greater redemption by delivering us from the slavery of sin through the Lamb of God, our Messiah. Blessed are You, O Lord, who sanctifies Israel and the festival seasons.

Drink the first cup of wine.

URCHATZ **HAND WASHING CEREMONY** וּרְחַץ

The leader only, using the basin of water and towel, washes his hands.

The seder plate elements

Leader: On our seder plate, we have six items which help to tell the Passover story. Each of these elements will add to our understanding of how God redeemed our people from Egypt, setting us free to serve Him.

KARPAS GREENS כַּרְפַּס

Leader: The *karpas*, or greens, remind us of the hyssop that was used to apply the blood of the Passover lambs to the homes of our ancestors in Egypt, sparing the lives of their firstborn sons. Green is also the color of life, the color of growing things, and these greens represent the life of our people in the land of Egypt.

The salt water represents the many tears shed by our ancestors when they were slaves in the land of Egypt. As we dip a sprig of the *karpas* into the salt water, we remember that a life without redemption is one that is filled with tears and sorrow.

All: Let us be grateful that we are redeemed by Y'shua and that while tears will surely come in this life, we have a promise of an eternity free of tears and sorrow.

Participants recite the blessing, dip the karpas into salt water and eat it.

בָּרוּךְ אַתָּה יְיָ, אֱלֹהֵינוּ מֶלֶךְ הָעוֹלָם, בּוֹרֵא פְּרִי הָאֲדָמָה:

Baruch atah Adonai, Elohenu melech ha-olam, borei p'ri ha-adamah.

Blessed are You, O Lord our God, King of the Universe, who creates the fruit of the earth.

Yachatz — Breaking the Middle Matzah   יַחַץ

Leader: (*Lifts up the matzah tash.*) This three-part pouch, the *matzah tash*, is also called a "unity." Each compartment of this unity contains a board of matzah. Some rabbis teach that this three in one unity represents the Patriarchs—Abraham, Isaac and Jacob. Others speculate that it represents the unity of worship in ancient Israel—the Priests, the Levites and the congregation. Still others see it as a unity of crowns—the crown of learning, the crown of the priesthood and the crown of kingship.

All: For believers in Y'shua, this unity speaks of the mystery of the tri-unity of God in Father, Son and Holy Spirit. One yet three. Three yet one.

Leader: We break the middle matzah in two (*breaks the matzah*) and return half to the *matzah tash*. The middle matzah that is removed is given a new name—the *afikoman*. It is wrapped in linen and hidden for a time. Later in the service, the children will search for it, and the one who finds it will receive a reward. It will need to be found for its special use.

The leader then instructs the children to close their eyes and hides the afikoman for later in the service.

Leader: (*Lifts up the remaining matzah on the plate.*) This is the bread of affliction that our ancestors ate in the land of Egypt. Then we were slaves, now we are free. Yet many of our Jewish people live in lands where persecution is all too common. Others fear for their safety. Still others are in need of basic necessities. Our God is a God of compassion and mercy and will meet all our needs in Y'shua.

All: Let all who are hungry come and eat of this bread and be filled. Let all come and freely celebrate the Passover.

Leader: And for those who do not have assurance that their sins are forgiven, it is our prayer that they come to know the freedom, peace and eternal life possible through Y'shua our Redeemer and truly be filled forever.

Leader sets down the matzah and the second cup is filled.

MA NISHTANAH   THE FOUR QUESTIONS   מַה נִּשְׁתַּנָּה

Traditionally, the youngest child in the family asks the four questions of the head of the house. More than one child can be chosen to share the honor if desired.

Child:

מַה נִּשְׁתַּנָּה הַלַּיְלָה הַזֶּה מִכָּל הַלֵּילוֹת?

שֶׁבְּכָל הַלֵּילוֹת, אָנוּ אוֹכְלִין חָמֵץ וּמַצָּה.
הַלַּיְלָה הַזֶּה כֻּלּוֹ מַצָּה:

שֶׁבְּכָל הַלֵּילוֹת, אָנוּ אוֹכְלִין שְׁאָר יְרָקוֹת.
הַלַּיְלָה הַזֶּה מָרוֹר:

שֶׁבְּכָל הַלֵּילוֹת, אָנוּ מַטְבִּילִין אֲפִלּוּ פַּעַם אֶחָת.
הַלַּיְלָה הַזֶּה שְׁתֵּי פְעָמִים:

שֶׁבְּכָל הַלֵּילוֹת, אָנוּ אוֹכְלִין בֵּין יוֹשְׁבִין וּבֵין מְסֻבִּין.
הַלַּיְלָה הַזֶּה כֻּלָּנוּ מְסֻבִּין:

Child: Mah nishtanah ha-lailah ha-zeh mikol haleilot?

She-b'chol ha-leilot, anu ochlin chametz u-matzah.
Ha-lailah ha-zeh kulo matzah.

She-b'chol ha-leilot, anu ochlin sh'ar y'rakot.
Ha-lailah hazeh kulo maror.

She-b'chol ha-leilot, ein anu matbilin, afilu pa'am echat.
Ha-lailah ha-zeh sh'tay f'a-mim.

She-b'chol ha-leilot, anu ochlin ben yoshvin u-ven m'subin.
Ha-lailah ha-zeh kulanu m'subin.

Child: Why is this night different from all other nights?

On all other nights we eat bread or matzah. Why on this night do we only eat matzah?
On all other nights we eat all sorts of vegetables. Why on this night do we eat bitter herbs?
On all other nights we do not dip our foods even once. Why on this night do we dip twice—*karpas* into salt water and *maror* into *charoset*?

On all other nights we either sit or recline at the dinner table. Why on this night do we only recline?

Leader: According to the Talmud,[1] when we stand before the judgment seat of God, He will have four questions for us.
Were we honest in business?
Did we make time to study His words of instruction?
Did we build up and encourage family life?
Have we hoped for our salvation?

May we come confidently to His throne knowing that we can answer that not only have each of us hoped in salvation but *have* that salvation in Y'shua who is the Blessed Hope, the Truth, the Living Word and the center of our family life.

Leader: As the story of the Exodus is now told, the children's questions will be answered.

MAGGID   TELLING THE EXODUS STORY   מַגִּיד

Reader 1: We were slaves under Pharaoh in Egypt and God set us free with a mighty hand and an outstretched arm. If the Lord our God had not delivered us from Egypt, we and our children, and our children's children, might still be slaves in Egypt to this very day. However, tonight we recount how our God rescued us.

Reader 2: Scripture records that there was a great famine in Canaan where Jacob and his family lived, so the sons of Jacob

1. Shabbat 31a.

traveled to Egypt to purchase food. Joseph, the favored son of Jacob, who had been hated by his brothers years earlier and sold into slavery, was not abandoned by God. He not only forgave his brothers for their treachery, but because of the favor and influence he had with Egypt's Pharaoh, his whole family was welcomed to live in the land of Egypt and was provided for during the times of famine.

Reader 1: And so our ancestors settled in Goshen and they watched their children grow tall, and their numbers grew strong. Life was pleasant and secure for many years. But a time came when a Pharaoh rose up who did not know Joseph, and he grew concerned that there were now more Hebrews than Egyptians living in the Land. Fearing our strength, he turned against us and made us his slaves.

Reader 2: He put taskmasters over our people, forcing us to build his storage cities. Despite the hard work and exhaustion, our people still grew in numbers. This enraged the Pharaoh even more. So he gave orders that every Jewish baby boy was to be drowned in the Nile River and thus eventually the entire nation would die!

Reader 1: Our people cried out to the Lord in their distress and He heard our cry. God looked on our pain and heard our groaning and He remembered His covenant with Abraham, and with Isaac and with Jacob. God looked on His people and He had great compassion. He raised up Moses, from the tribe of Levi, to lead us out of Egypt and into the Promised Land. Deliverance was close at hand.

Eser Makkot　　The Ten Plagues　　עֶשֶׂר מַכּוֹת

Reader 2: God appeared to His servant Moses in the midst of a burning bush. And He told Moses to go to Pharaoh and tell him to set our people free. Fearful though he was, Moses obeyed. But Pharaoh thought he was more powerful than the One who sent Moses, so he said "no"—not once, but ten times! Pharaoh's "no's" were met by ten plagues on the land of Egypt. Each one was worse than the one before it.

Reader 1: Though protected from the first nine plagues, the Israelites needed God's special provision to be spared from the tenth plague, the slaying of the firstborn sons! God told Moses to have each Israelite household sacrifice a perfect lamb—a lamb without spot or blemish—a yearling lamb from among the males. The bones of this lamb were not to be broken. And God commanded the people:

"Eat it in haste; it is the LORD'S Passover." (Exodus 12:11)

Reader 2: With hyssop, the blood of this sacrificial lamb was to be placed on the doorposts of the home where it was eaten. And God said:

"On that same night I will pass through Egypt and strike down every firstborn—both men and animals—and I will bring judgment on all the gods of Egypt. I am the LORD." (Exodus 12:12)

The firstborn sons living in the homes that were covered with the blood of the lamb were spared, for God passed over those who were obedient to His word. This is where we get the name of the holiday: *Pesach* or Passover.

| **Kos Makkot** | **The Cup of Plagues** | כּוֹס מַכּוֹת |

Lift the second cup.

Leader: In Jewish tradition, a full cup is a symbol of complete joy. We do not rejoice that our enemies had to suffer plagues and die in order for us to be set free, so we make the cup less than full by removing a drop of wine from our cups for each of the ten plagues, as we recite them in both Hebrew and English:

Dam	Blood	דָּם
Tz'farde'ah	Frogs	צְפַרְדֵּעַ
Kinim	Lice	כִּנִּים
Arov	Wild beasts	עָרוֹב
Dever	Disease	דֶּבֶר
Sh'chin	Boils	שְׁחִין
Barad	Hail	בָּרָד
Arbeh	Locusts	אַרְבֶּה
Choshech	Darkness	חֹשֶׁךְ
Makat b'chorot	Slaying of the Firstborn	מַכַּת בְּכוֹרוֹת

Leader: The Lord has been generous to overflowing in all He has done for us. Any of His many saving acts would be enough for us to shout out our thanks and offer our praise to Him.

Leader: If He had only taken us out of Egypt and not judged the Egyptians:

All: Dayenu! It would have been enough!

Leader: If He had judged their gods, but not slain the firstborn:

All: Dayenu! It would have been enough!

Leader: If He had divided the Red Sea but not allowed us to pass through on to dry ground:

All: Dayenu! It would have been enough!

Leader: If He allowed us to pass, but did not drown the Egyptian's armies:

All: Dayenu! It would have been enough!

Leader: If He had brought us into the wilderness but not fed us with manna:

All: Dayenu! It would have been enough!

Leader: If He had fed us with manna but not given us the Sabbath:

All: Dayenu! It would have been enough!

Leader: If He had given us the Sabbath but not the Torah:

All: Dayenu! It would have been enough!

Leader: If He had given us the Torah but had not led us into Israel:

All: Dayenu! It would have been enough!

Leader: If He had given us Israel but not built and consecrated the Temple:

All: Dayenu! It would have been enough!

Leader: As followers of Y'shua, we add still another Dayenu. Our God not only provided all the above, He provided a once and for all atonement for us through Jesus the Messiah who died for our sins and rose from the dead so that we can know freedom from sin and abundant life now and forever. And for this we can all say:

All: Dayenu! It is indeed enough!

Song: Dayenu

אִלוּ, אִלוּ הוֹצִיאָנוּ, הוֹצִיאָנוּ מִמִּצְרַיִם, הוֹצִיאָנוּ מִמִּצְרַיִם,
דַּיֵּנוּ! דַּי דַּיֵּנוּ, דַּי דַּיֵּנוּ, דַּי דַּיֵּנוּ, דַּיֵּנוּ, דַּיֵּנוּ!

אִלוּ נָתַן, נָתַן לָנוּ, נָתַן לָנוּ אֶת־הַשַּׁבָּת,
נָתַן לָנוּ אֶת־הַשַּׁבָּת, דַּיֵּנוּ!...

אִלוּ נָתַן, נָתַן לָנוּ, נָתַן לָנוּ אֶת־הַתּוֹרָה,
נָתַן לָנוּ אֶת־הַתּוֹרָה, דַּיֵּנוּ!...

אִלוּ נָתַן, נָתַן לָנוּ, נָתַן לָנוּ אֶת־יֵשׁוּעַ,
נָתַן לָנוּ אֶת־יֵשׁוּעַ, דַּיֵּנוּ!...

Ilu ilu hotzianu, hotzianu mi mitzrayim,
hotzianu mi mitzrayim, Dayenu!

Chorus:
> *Dai, Dayenu, Dai, Dayenu, Dai, Dayenu, Dayenu, Dayenu!*

Ilu natan, natan lanu, natan lanu et ha-Shabbat,
Natan lanu et ha-Shabbat, Dayenu!

(Chorus)

Ilu natan, natan lanu, natan lanu et ha-Torah,
Natan lanu et ha-Torah, Dayenu!

(Chorus)

Ilu natan, natan lanu, natan lanu et Y'shua
Natan lanu et Y'shua, Dayenu!

(Chorus)

For sheet music and download information for mp3s, see page 59.

The Three Symbols Of Passover

Leader: Rabbi Gamaliel said that in order to tell the Passover story properly, we must mention three important things. *Pesach*, matzah and *maror*—the Passover Lamb, the unleavened bread and the bitter herbs.

Reader 2: The Passover Lamb was God's provision for our people in ancient Egypt. John called Y'shua the Lamb of God who takes away the sins of the world. Y'shua was God's perfect lamb sacrificed for us. As our ancestors applied the blood of the Passover lamb to the doorposts of their homes, sparing the firstborn sons from death, today we apply the blood of Y'shua, God's lamb, to the doorposts of our hearts through faith. When we do this, we are forgiven of our sin and are set free to serve the living God.

Reader 1: We eat the matzah, the unleavened bread, as our ancestors did when God took them out of Egypt in haste and there was no time to wait for their bread to rise. The matzah is like our Messiah Y'shua, who was without leaven, without sin. The piercing and stripes on the matzah bring to mind the words of the prophet Isaiah who said of Y'shua:

"But he was pierced for our transgressions, he was crushed for our iniquities; the punishment that brought us peace was upon him, and by his stripes we are healed" (Isaiah 53:5).

Our ancestors ate manna in the wilderness as they left Egypt for the Promised Land. We are offered the bread of life, Y'shua, to satisfy us forever.

Reader 2: This bitter herb or *maror*, reminds us of the embittered life that our people endured as slaves in Egypt. The bitter root, *chazeret*, reminds us that bitterness goes down to the root of our very being and cannot merely be topped off. We are all slaves to sin and bitterness and we will never know the sweetness of freedom until we let the Messiah Jesus uproot the sin in our lives and set us free.

Leader: In every generation, we are to see ourselves as though we personally came out of slavery in Egypt. For God not only redeemed our ancestors, He redeemed us too, and for this reason we praise Him.

Raise the second cup and say:

All: We praise You, O Lord, for bringing us from bondage to freedom, from despair to hope, from sorrow to joy, from darkness to Your great light.

Put down the second cup and continue with psalms of praise:

PSALMS OF PRAISE 113-115

Leader: Praise the LORD. Praise, O servants of the LORD, praise the name of the LORD.

All: Let the name of the LORD be praised, both now and forevermore.

Leader: From the rising of the sun to the place where it sets, the name of the LORD is to be praised.

All: The LORD is exalted over all the nations, his glory above the heavens.

Leader: Who is like the LORD our God, the One who sits enthroned on high,

All: Who stoops down to look on the heavens and the earth?

Leader: He raises the poor from the dust and lifts the needy from the ash heap;

All: He seats them with princes, with the princes of their people.

Leader: He settles the barren woman in her home as a happy mother of children. Praise the LORD.

All: When Israel came out of Egypt, the house of Jacob from a people of foreign tongue,

Leader: Judah became God's sanctuary, Israel his dominion.

All: The sea looked and fled, the Jordan turned back;

Leader: The mountains skipped like rams, the hills like lambs.

All: Why was it, O sea, that you fled, O Jordan, that you turned back,

Leader: You mountains, that you skipped like rams, you hills, like lambs?

All: Tremble, O earth, at the presence of the Lord, at the presence of the God of Jacob,

Leader: Who turned the rock into a pool, the hard rock into springs of water.

All: Not to us, O LORD, not to us but to your name be the glory, because of your love and faithfulness.

Leader: Why do the nations say, "Where is their God?"

All: Our God is in heaven; he does whatever pleases him.

Leader: But their idols are silver and gold, made by the hands of men.

All: They have mouths, but cannot speak, eyes, but they cannot see;

Leader: They have ears, but cannot hear, noses, but they cannot smell;

All: They have hands, but cannot feel, feet, but they cannot walk; nor can they utter a sound with their throats.

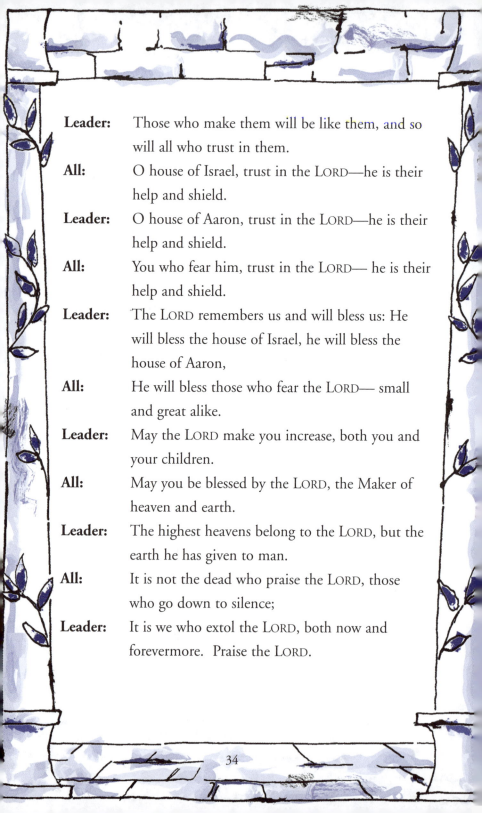

Leader: Those who make them will be like them, and so will all who trust in them.

All: O house of Israel, trust in the LORD—he is their help and shield.

Leader: O house of Aaron, trust in the LORD—he is their help and shield.

All: You who fear him, trust in the LORD— he is their help and shield.

Leader: The LORD remembers us and will bless us: He will bless the house of Israel, he will bless the house of Aaron,

All: He will bless those who fear the LORD— small and great alike.

Leader: May the LORD make you increase, both you and your children.

All: May you be blessed by the LORD, the Maker of heaven and earth.

Leader: The highest heavens belong to the LORD, but the earth he has given to man.

All: It is not the dead who praise the LORD, those who go down to silence;

Leader: It is we who extol the LORD, both now and forevermore. Praise the LORD.

We now raise the second cup again and say:

All: We bless you O Lord, our King and our Redeemer. We praise you, O Lord, for not only redeeming our ancestors from the slavery of Egypt but for sending the ultimate Deliverer in Y'shua, who frees us from sin and death. For it is written, "For God so loved the world that he gave his one and only Son, that whoever believes in him will not perish but have eternal life" (John 3:16).

בָּרוּךְ אַתָּה יְיָ, אֱלֹהֵינוּ מֶלֶךְ הָעוֹלָם, בּוֹרֵא פְּרִי הַגָּפֶן:

Baruch atah Adonai, Elohenu melech ha-olam, borei p'ri ha-gafen.

Blessed are You, O Lord our God, King of the Universe, who creates the fruit of the vine.

We drink the second cup.

PREPARING FOR THE MEAL

RACHTZAH **WASHING THE HANDS**   רָחְצָה

Leader: In preparation for eating the Passover meal, we wash our hands by passing a basin, pitcher and towel to the person seated next to us. We help one another in the process. However, Y'shua took this tradition a step further:

. . . so he got up from the meal, took off his outer clothing, and wrapped a towel around his waist. After that, he poured water into a basin and began to wash his disciples' feet, drying them with the towel that was wrapped around him. (John 13: 4, 5)

Leader: The Lord set the example for us to serve one another at Passover when He said:

". . . the greatest among you should be like the youngest, and the one who rules like the one who serves." (Luke 22:26)

Reader 1: We will now say the blessing and wash one another's hands in preparation for the meal:

בָּרוּךְ אַתָּה יְיָ, אֱלֹהֵינוּ מֶלֶךְ הָעוֹלָם, אֲשֶׁר קִדְּשָׁנוּ
בְּמִצְוֹתָיו וְצִוָּנוּ עַל נְטִילַת יָדָיִם:

Baruch atah Adonai, Elohenu melech ha-olam, asher kid'shanu b'mitzvotav v'tzivanu al n'tilat yadayim.

Blessed are You, O Lord our God, King of the Universe, who has sanctified us by Your commandments and commanded us to wash our hands.

Motzi Matzah   Blessing over the Matzah   מוֹצִיא מַצָּה

The top piece of matzah in the matzah tash is distributed to all present along with the remaining portion of the center piece, which was not hidden earlier.

Leader: The top and bottom pieces of matzah symbolize our physical need for bread to sustain us. The center piece is symbolic of the living bread, Y'shua, who spiritually makes us whole.

A piece of the top and center piece of matzah should be passed around to everyone at the table. Chant the blessings and eat:

בָּרוּךְ אַתָּה יְיָ, אֱלֹהֵינוּ מֶלֶךְ הָעוֹלָם, הַמּוֹצִיא לֶחֶם מִן הָאָרֶץ:

Baruch atah Adonai, Elohenu melech ha-olam, ha-motzi lechem min ha-aretz.

Blessed are You, O Lord our God, King of the Universe, who brings forth bread from the earth.

בָּרוּךְ אַתָּה יְיָ אֱלֹהֵינוּ מֶלֶךְ הָעוֹלָם, אֲשֶׁר קִדְּשָׁנוּ
בְּמִצְוֹתָיו וְצִוָּנוּ עַל אֲכִילַת מַצָּה:

Baruch atah Adonai, Elohenu melech ha-olam, asher kid'shanu b'mitzvotav v'tzivanu al achilat matzah.

Blessed are You, O Lord our God, King of the Universe, who has sanctified us by Your commandments and commanded us to eat unleavened bread.

MAROR   **BITTER HERBS**   מָרוֹר

Leader: We will now eat of the *maror*. Its bitter taste reminds us of the bitterness of slavery. Our rabbis say that we need to eat at least a tablespoon to truly feel the bitterness, to produce some tears, but we'll leave the amount up to you, as long as you take enough to get a good taste!

Dip matzah in bitter herbs and say:

בָּרוּךְ אַתָּה יְיָ אֱלֹהֵינוּ מֶלֶךְ הָעוֹלָם, אֲשֶׁר קִדְּשָׁנוּ
בְּמִצְוֹתָיו וְצִוָּנוּ עַל אֲכִילַת מָרוֹר:

Baruch atah Adonai, Elohenu melech ha-olam, asher kid'shanu b'mitzvotav v'tzivanu al achilat maror.

Blessed are You, O Lord our God, King of the Universe, who has sanctified us by Your commandments and commanded us to eat *maror*, the bitter herbs.

| **CHAROSET** | **SWEET FRUIT MIXTURE** | חֲרֹסֶת |

Leader: We dip the matzah into the *charoset*. The *charoset* is a sweet mixture, yet it symbolizes the mortar that went into building the storage cities for Pharaoh. The reason it is so sweet is that God wanted us to remember that even the bitterest of our labors can be sweet, when we know His redemption is near. Let us eat.

| **KORECH** | **THE HILLEL SANDWICH** | כּוֹרֵךְ |

Leader: The original Hillel sandwich was taken with some roasted lamb, bitter herbs and matzah to remind us of the essential ingredients of the Passover. After the destruction of the Temple, lamb was no longer to be eaten at the seder according to the rabbis, but to meet in a small measure this requirement, today we combine the bitter herbs with the sweet *charoset*. The *charoset* sweetens the bitterness of the *maror*, just as God's redemption brings sweetness to our lives. The *charoset* also reminds us that life is filled with both the bitter and the sweet, with sorrow and joy, with mourning and dancing. Let us eat together.

| **BEITZAH** | **ROASTED EGG** | בֵּיצָה |

Leader: (*Holds up the egg.*) This *beitzah* is roasted to remind us of the *chagigah*, the festival sacrifice made at the Temple in Jerusalem. It is now a symbol of sadness and grief to our people because the Temple no longer stands and there is no physical place to sacrifice and make atonement for our sins. The prophet Daniel predicted Messiah would first have to die as our sacrifice and shortly after that the Temple would be destroyed. Y'shua died for us about A.D. 32 and in A.D. 70 the Temple was destroyed. But we rejoice because Messiah came as the final *chagigah* for sin and He is the Living Temple. Hallelujah! Since there's no longer reason for us to shed tears of despair today, let us dip the egg in salt water to symbolize our tears of joy at Y'shua's provision.

Eat the egg dipped in salt water.

SHULCHAN ORECH   THE SEDER MEAL   שֻׁלְחָן עוֹרֵךְ

After the meal, all the children search for the hidden afikoman. When the afikoman is recovered, the leader gives an appropriate reward to the child who discovered its hiding place.

The third cup is filled at this time as well.

AFIKOMAN   THAT WHICH COMES AFTER   צָפוּן

Leader: *Afikoman* means "that which comes after," or "that which makes things complete." According to others, it means "the coming one" and refers to the coming Messiah. We can't complete our seder without it. The *afikoman* was the bread that Y'shua gave His disciples after their Passover meal. He told them to take and eat it for it represented His body that would be broken for us. This bread is our Messiah's gift to us. He promised that whoever comes to Him will never go hungry and whoever believes in Him will never be thirsty (John 6:35).

בָּרוּךְ אַתָּה, יְיָ אֱלֹהֵינוּ מֶלֶךְ הָעוֹלָם, הַמּוֹצִיא לֶחֶם מִן הָאָרֶץ:

Baruch atah Adonai, Elohenu melech ha-olam, ha-motzi lechem min ha-aretz.

Blessed are You, O Lord our God, King of the Universe, who brings forth bread from the earth.

בָּרוּךְ אַתָּה, יְיָ אֱלֹהֵינוּ מֶלֶךְ הָעוֹלָם, הַמּוֹצִיא לֶחֶם מִן הַשָּׁמַיִם:

Baruch atah Adonai, Elohenu melech ha-olam, ha-motzi lechem min ha-shamayim.

Blessed are You, O Lord our God, King of the Universe, who brings forth bread from heaven.

Let us eat the *afikoman* together.

Nothing further is eaten at the traditional seder after this.

Kos G'ulah   The Cup of Redemption   כּוֹס גְּאֻלָּה

Leader: In the same way, Y'shua took the cup of redemption. He said the blessing over it and passed it among the disciples. He said that this cup was the new covenant, or agreement, between God and our people, sealed in His blood. He said that as often as we would do this, we would be remembering what He did for us when He shed His blood for our sins. Let us chant the blessing together and then take the third cup.

בָּרוּךְ אַתָּה יְיָ, אֱלֹהֵינוּ מֶלֶךְ הָעוֹלָם, בּוֹרֵא פְּרִי הַגָּפֶן:

Baruch atah Adonai, Elohenu melech ha-olam, borei p'ri ha-gafen.

Blessed are You, O Lord our God, King of the Universe, who creates the fruit of the vine.

Drink the third cup of wine.

SONG: ETERNALLY GRATEFUL

I am eternally grateful to Jesus,
For all He has done for me.
He has given me life and salvation,
Given me liberty.

Chorus:
>Oh, Lord I praise and I bless Your name,
>Give the glory to You, to You.
>My heart, my soul they're in Your hands,
>Teach me to worship You.

I will lift up the cup of salvation,
And call upon His Name.

Through His blood I have redemption,
A brand new life I claim.

(Chorus)

Bless the Lord, bless the Lord, oh my soul,
And all that's within my frame,
Join and sing out the praises of Jesus,
Eternal, forever the same.

(Chorus)

Words and music by Janie-sue Wertheim, Copyright © 1979
For sheet music and download information for mp3s, see page 59.

BARECH   GRACE AFTER THE MEAL

All: We thank you, O Lord, for providing this food we have eaten that nourishes our bodies. We thank you, O Lord, as well for providing the *afikoman* and the Cup of Redemption, which nourishes our souls.

Leader: Blessed are You, O Lord our God, who provides for the whole world in Your goodness. It is You who provides for all, sustains all and is all sufficient for the needs of Your creation.

All: We thank You for Your lovingkindness and grace and mercy which you bestow on us continually, every day, and at every season and in every moment of each hour.

Leader: Blessed be our God whose gifts we have enjoyed and by whose goodness we live.

All: O taste and see that the Lord is good.

Leader: How blessed is the one who takes refuge in Him!

All: O fear the Lord, you His saints.

Leader: Those who fear Him lack no good thing.

All: The young lions do lack and suffer hunger.

Leader: But they who seek the Lord shall not be in want of any good thing (Psalm 34:8-10).

Fill the fourth cup.
The leader then raises the Cup of Elijah.

Leader: In Jewish tradition, Elijah the prophet is expected to come at Passover and to herald the Messiah's coming. We know from the words of the prophet Malachi, that Elijah would usher in that great and terrible day of the Lord. And so we set out a place at the Passover table for him each year. And we open the door to our home, hoping that Elijah will be there so we can invite him in.

A child is sent to the front entrance of the home and opens the door.

Leader: For those of us who know Messiah, we know that one came 2,000 years ago in the power and spirit of Elijah to announce the coming of Messiah. John or Yochanon, known as the baptizer, heralded Y'shua with these words, "Look, the Lamb of God, who takes away the sin of the world" (John 1:29)! Even today, our Messiah Himself stands at the door of our hearts and says, "Here I am! I stand at the door and knock. If anyone hears my voice and opens the door, I will come in and eat with him, and he with me" (Revelation 3:20). Jesus invites us to come to Him and enjoy the peace that only His presence can bring to our hearts.

Song: Eliyahu Ha-Navi

אֵלִיָהוּ הַנָבִיא, אֵלִיָהוּ הַתִּשְׁבִּי, אֵלִיָהוּ, אֵלִיָהוּ, אֵלִיָהוּ
הַגִּלְעָדִי. בִּמְהֵרָה בְיָמֵינוּ יָבֹא אֵלֵינוּ, עִם מָשִׁיחַ
בֶּן דָוִד, עִם מָשִׁיחַ בֶּן דָוִד.

Eliyahu ha-navi, Eliyahu ha-Tishbi,
Eliyahu, Eliyahu, Eliyahu ha-Giladi

Bimherah v'yamenu
Yavo eleinu,
im Mashiach ben David,
im Mashiach ben David.

Eliyahu ha-navi, Eliyahu ha-Tishbi,
Eliyahu, Eliyahu, Eliyahu ha-Giladi.

Traditional. For sheet music and download information for mp3s, see page 59.

Translation:
Elijah the Prophet, Elijah the Tishbite,
Elijah, Elijah, Elijah the Gileadite
Speedily and in our days, come to us,
With the Messiah, son of David,
With the Messiah, son of David.

A child then closes the door.

Leader: We continue in praise to our God by reciting the remainder of the Hallel Psalms. Y'shua and His disciples might have been reciting them as well at this point in the seder.

PSALMS OF PRAISE 116-118

Leader: I love the LORD, for he heard my voice; he heard my cry for mercy.

All: Because he turned his ear to me, I will call on him as long as I live.

Leader: The cords of death entangled me, the anguish of the grave came upon me; I was overcome by trouble and sorrow.

All: Then I called on the name of the LORD: "O LORD, save me!"

Leader: The LORD is gracious and righteous; our God is full of compassion.

All: The LORD protects the simplehearted; when I was in great need, he saved me.

Leader: Be at rest once more, O my soul, for the LORD has been good to you.

All: For you, O LORD, have delivered my soul from death, my eyes from tears, my feet from stumbling,

Leader: That I may walk before the LORD in the land of the living.

All: I believed; therefore I said, "I am greatly afflicted."

Leader: And in my dismay I said, "All men are liars."

All: How can I repay the LORD for all his goodness to me?

Leader: I will lift up the cup of salvation and call on the name of the LORD.

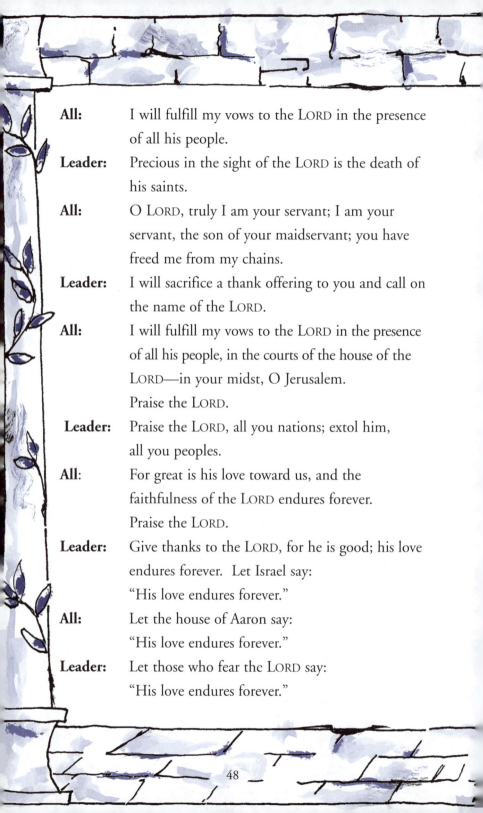

All: I will fulfill my vows to the LORD in the presence of all his people.

Leader: Precious in the sight of the LORD is the death of his saints.

All: O LORD, truly I am your servant; I am your servant, the son of your maidservant; you have freed me from my chains.

Leader: I will sacrifice a thank offering to you and call on the name of the LORD.

All: I will fulfill my vows to the LORD in the presence of all his people, in the courts of the house of the LORD—in your midst, O Jerusalem.
Praise the LORD.

Leader: Praise the LORD, all you nations; extol him, all you peoples.

All: For great is his love toward us, and the faithfulness of the LORD endures forever.
Praise the LORD.

Leader: Give thanks to the LORD, for he is good; his love endures forever. Let Israel say:
"His love endures forever."

All: Let the house of Aaron say:
"His love endures forever."

Leader: Let those who fear the LORD say:
"His love endures forever."

All: In my anguish I cried to the L ORD, and he answered by setting me free.

Leader: The L ORD is with me; I will not be afraid. What can man do to me?

All: The L ORD is with me; he is my helper. I will look in triumph on my enemies. It is better to take refuge in the L ORD than to trust in man.

Leader: It is better to take refuge in the L ORD than to trust in princes.

All: All the nations surrounded me, but in the name of the L ORD I cut them off.

Leader: They surrounded me on every side, but in the name of the L ORD I cut them off.

All: They swarmed around me like bees, but they died out as quickly as burning thorns; in the name of the L ORD I cut them off.

Leader: I was pushed back and about to fall, but the L ORD helped me.

All: The L ORD is my strength and my song; he has become my salvation.

Leader: Shouts of joy and victory resound in the tents of the righteous: "The L ORD'S right hand has done mighty things!

All: The L ORD'S right hand is lifted high; the L ORD'S right hand has done mighty things!"

Leader: I will not die but live,
and will proclaim what the Lord has done.
All: The Lord has chastened me severely,
but he has not given me over to death.
Leader: Open for me the gates of righteousness;
I will enter and give thanks to the Lord.
All: This is the gate of the Lord
through which the righteous may enter.
Leader: I will give you thanks, for you answered me; you have become my salvation.
All: The stone the builders rejected has become the capstone;
Leader: The Lord has done this, and it is marvelous in our eyes.
All: This is the day the Lord has made; let us rejoice and be glad in it.
Leader: O Lord, save us; O Lord, grant us success.
All: Blessed is he who comes in the name of the Lord. From the house of the Lord we bless you.
Leader: The Lord is God, and he has made his light shine upon us. With boughs in hand, join in the festal procession up to the horns of the altar.
All: You are my God, and I will give you thanks; you are my God, and I will exalt you. Give thanks to the Lord, for he is good; his love endures forever.

Hallel   Cup of Praise   הַלֵּל

Leader: The fourth and final cup is the Hallel, or cup of praise. We praise God for His marvelous work of redeeming us out of slavery in Egypt, but even more, for freeing us from being slaves to sin through Y'shua's death and resurrection. Lord, we will give praise to Your name forever. You are our King, enthroned, high and exalted and we delight in speaking Your praise.

Leader: Let us chant the blessing over the wine.

בָּרוּךְ אַתָּה יְיָ, אֱלֹהֵינוּ מֶלֶךְ הָעוֹלָם, בּוֹרֵא פְּרִי הַגָּפֶן:

Baruch atah Adonai, Elohenu melech ha-olam, borei p'ri ha-gafen.

Blessed are You, O Lord our God, King of the Universe, who creates the fruit of the vine.

Drink the fourth cup of wine.

Leader: Let us continue in the singing of God's praises, for it is our duty and joy to offer praise in psalm and hymn and song. The Hallel service is a time when we can offer abundant praise to our God for He is worthy of all praise, honor, glory and thanksgiving!

You can intersperse traditional Passover songs (starting on page 60) throughout this portion of the service. See also page 59 for download information for mp3s of the following English songs.

SONG: PRAISE AND GLORY (PSALM 92)

It is good to praise you Lord,
And make music to your name,
Proclaim your love in the morning,
And your faithfulness at night.

Chorus:

>Praise and glory and wisdom and thanks,
>Honor and power and strength,
>Be to our God forever and ever, be to our God, Amen.

You make me glad by your deeds,
I sing for joy at the work of your hands,
How great are your works O Lord,
How profound are your thoughts.

(Chorus)

Make me like a palm tree my God,
That I may flourish in your courts all my life,
And bear fruit even when I grow old,
You only are my rock!

(Chorus 2x)

Words and music by Stephen Katz, Copyright © 1991.

Song: Come and Praise the Lord (Psalm 118)

Give thanks to the Lord for His goodness,
His faithful love endureth forever.

Chorus:
>Come and praise the Lord,
>Come and praise the Lord,
>For His mercy is wondrous in our eyes *(2x)*
>Hallelujah, Hallelujah,
>Hallelu, Hallelujah *(2x)*

In my trouble I asked Him to save me,
He answered and set me in safety.

(Chorus)

The Lord, my Redeemer, is for me,
No more can the wicked destroy me.

(Chorus)

The stone which the builders rejected,
The Lord has made the cornerstone for all.

(Chorus)

>*Words and music by Steffi Geiser Rubin/Stuart Dauermann,*
>*Copyright ©1982. Lillenas.*

Song: Worthy to be Praised

He loves us as we are and He takes us in.
Fills our aching hearts and frees us from our sin.

Chorus:
>   And He's worthy to be praised.
>   Yes He's worthy to be obeyed.
>   Deserving the best that our hearts can give.
>   Worthy to be praised.

God sent the very best then put Him to the test.
He suffered on that tree but then rose in victory.

(Chorus)

He gave me a song that the angels can't sing.
I have been redeemed by the Lamb who was slain.

(Chorus)

>   Words and music by Janie-sue Wertheim, Copyright ©1982. 1990.

Leader:	Praise the Lord!
All:	Praise the Lord from the heavens; Praise Him in the heights!
Leader:	Praise Him, all His angels; Praise Him, all His hosts!
All:	Praise Him, sun and moon; Praise Him, all you stars of light!

Leader: Praise Him, you heavens of heavens,
And you waters above the heavens!
All: Let everyone praise the name of the Lord
For His name alone is exalted;
His glory is above the earth and heaven.
Leader: And He has exalted the horn of His people,
The praise of all His saints—
Of the children of Israel,
A people near to Him.
All: Praise the Lord!

Leader: And as we praise Him, we also sing with the hope that He will return soon. Next year may it be the will of the Lord that we celebrate Passover in peace with our family and friends in the holy city, even in the New Jerusalem! L'shana ha-ba'ah bi-rushalyim. Next year in Jerusalem.

Song: L'shanah Ha-Ba'ah Bi-rushalayim

לְשָׁנָה הַבָּאָה בִּירוּשָׁלָיִם!

L'shanah ha-ba'ah bi-rushalayim!
L'shanah ha-ba'ah bi-rushalayim!
L'shanah ha-ba'ah bi-rushalayim!
L'shanah ha-ba'ah bi-rushalayim!

Next Year in Jerusalem!

Traditional. See page 59 for sheet music.

Nirtzah   Our Seder Concludes   נִרְצָה

Leader: Then I saw a new heaven and a new earth, for the first heaven and the first earth had passed away, and there was no longer any sea. I saw the Holy City, the new Jerusalem, coming down out of heaven from God, prepared as a bride beautifully dressed for her husband. And I heard a loud voice from the throne saying, "Now the dwelling of God is with men, and he will live with them. They will be his people, and God himself will be with them and be their God. He will wipe every tear from their eyes. There will be no more death or mourning or crying or pain, for the old order of things has passed away" (Revelation 21:1-4).

This description is more than wishful thinking. We serve a living God who is not limited by time and space. The psalmist says that a thousand years in God's sight are like a day that has just gone by or like a watch in the night. And while we don't know when Messiah will return, we are confident that the day is coming. And we live in the hope of that reality. And that is why we can sing with anticipation and assurance, "Come Y'shua!"

Song: Come Y'shua

Chorus:

    Come Y'shua, Y'shua come.
    Hope for all ages is in the Son.
    Come Y'shua, Y'shua come.
    Come Y'shua, come.

  The prophets of old Messiah foretold.
  The dead will rise and we will meet our Lord.
  Soon he will come, God's righteous one.
  We will live with him forevermore.

(Chorus)

  The prophets of old Messiah foretold.
  He'll appear and Israel will see
  The nail prints in His hands.
  They'll mourn throughout the Land
  Cleansed, restored for all eternity.

(Chorus)

  The prophets of old Messiah foretold.
  He will rule the earth as Lord and King.
  Forever He'll reign, we'll all praise His name.
  Let us lift up our hearts to Him and sing.
  Let us sing.

(Chorus)

Words and music by Jonathan Sacks, Copyright ©1990.
For sheet music and download information for mp3s see page 59.

PASSOVER MUSIC RESOURCES

Sheet music for these traditional Passover songs can be found in a variety of publications. These include some of the more elaborate haggadot (such as those published by the Jewish Publication Society – JPS) and in music books such as *The World's Most Popular Passover Songs* (by Tara Publications, available for purchase online at http://www.jewishmusic.com/). This book contains 19 Passover songs. Those who want to hear the tunes can find downloadable versions of many of these songs by searching on the song title and "mp3" on a standard search engine. For starters, the site http://www.jewfaq.org/holidaya.htm#music offers simple recordings of four Passover songs, including *Ma Nishtana* (The Four Questions), *Dayenu, Eliyahu Hanavi* and *Adir Hu*.

To hear the melodies for the Messianic songs included in this Haggadah (*Eternally Grateful, Praise and Glory, Come and Praise the Lord, Worthy to be Praised* and *Come Y'shua*) go to jewsforjesus.org/mfhsongs to access a downloadable mp3.

ADDITIONAL SONG SERVICE

Adir Hu

אַדִּיר הוּא, אַדִּיר הוּא, יִבְנֶה בֵיתוֹ בְּקָרוֹב.
בִּמְהֵרָה, בִּמְהֵרָה, בְּיָמֵינוּ, בְּקָרוֹב.
אֵל בְּנֵה, אֵל בְּנֵה, בְּנֵה בֵיתְךָ בְּקָרוֹב!

בָּחוּר הוּא, גָּדוֹל הוּא, דָּגוּל הוּא, יִבְנֶה בֵיתוֹ בְּקָרוֹב...
הָדוּר הוּא, וָתִיק הוּא, זַכַּאי הוּא, יִבְנֶה בֵיתוֹ בְּקָרוֹב...
חָסִיד הוּא, טָהוֹר הוּא, יָחִיד הוּא, יִבְנֶה בֵיתוֹ בְּקָרוֹב...
כַּבִּיר הוּא, לָמוּד הוּא, מֶלֶךְ הוּא, יִבְנֶה בֵיתוֹ בְּקָרוֹב...
נָאוֹר הוּא, סַגִּיב הוּא, עִזּוּז הוּא, יִבְנֶה בֵיתוֹ בְּקָרוֹב...
פּוֹדֶה הוּא, צַדִּיק הוּא, קָדוֹשׁ הוּא, יִבְנֶה בֵיתוֹ בְּקָרוֹב...
רַחוּם הוּא, שַׁדַּי הוּא, תַּקִּיף הוּא, יִבְנֶה בֵיתוֹ בְּקָרוֹב...

Translation:

Adir hu, adir hu | May He who is most mighty
Yivneh veito b'karov; | soon rebuild His house;

Chorus:

    Bimherah, bimherah, — speedily, speedily,
    B'yamenu b'karov; — soon in our days;
    El b'neh, El b'neh, — O God, rebuild it
    B'neh veitcha b'karov. — rebuild Your house soon.

Bachur hu, gadol hu, dagul hu — May He who is chosen, great and distinguished

Yivneh veito b'karov — soon rebuild His house;

Chorus:

Bimherah, bimherah	speedily, speedily,
B'yamenu b'karov	soon in our days;
El b'neh, El b'neh	O God, rebuild it
B'neh veitcha b'karov	rebuild Your house soon.

Hadur hu, vatik hu, zakay hu — May He who is glorious, ancient and just

Yivneh veito b'karov — soon rebuild His house;

(Chorus)

Chasid hu, tahor hu, yachid[2] hu — May He who is gracious, pure and One

Yivneh veito b'karov — soon rebuild His house;

(Chorus)

Kabir hu, lamud hu, melech hu — May He who is powerful, learned and King

Yivneh veito b'karov — soon rebuild His house;

(Chorus)

Na'or hu, sagiv hu, izuz hu — May He who is awesome, sublime and powerful

Yivneh veito b'karov — soon rebuild His house;

2. *Yachid*, like *echad*, means "one" but is not used of God in the Bible. It has been used in traditional Judaism since the Middle Ages, and implies that God is singly one. *Echad* by contrast can allow for God to be three-in-one. In this song, and in *Ki Lo Na'eh*, the attributes of God that are named form an alphabetic acrostic in Hebrew, and we retain the traditional *yachid* wording in order to preserve the poetry.

(Chorus)

| Podeh hu, tzaddik hu, kadosh hu | May He who is Redeemer, righteous and holy |
| Yivneh veito b'karov | soon rebuild His house; |

(Chorus)

| Rachum hu, shaddai hu, takif hu | May He who is merciful, Almighty and strong |
| Yivneh veito b'karov | soon rebuild His house; |

CHAD GADYA

חַד גַּדְיָא, חַד גַּדְיָא. דְּזַבִּין אַבָּא בִּתְרֵי זוּזֵי. חַד גַּדְיָא, חַד גַּדְיָא.

וְאָתָא שׁוּנְרָא וְאָכְלָה לְגַדְיָא, דְּזַבִּין אַבָּא בִּתְרֵי זוּזֵי...

וְאָתָא כַלְבָּא וְנָשַׁךְ לְשׁוּנְרָא, דְּאָכְלָה לְגַדְיָא, דְּזַבִּין אַבָּא בִּתְרֵי זוּזֵי...

וְאָתָא חוּטְרָא וְהִכָּה לְכַלְבָּא, דְּנָשַׁךְ לְשׁוּנְרָא, דְּאָכְלָה לְגַדְיָא, דְּזַבִּין אַבָּא בִּתְרֵי זוּזֵי...

וְאָתָא נוּרָא וְשָׂרַף לְחוּטְרָא, דְּהִכָּה לְכַלְבָּא, דְּנָשַׁךְ לְשׁוּנְרָא, דְּאָכְלָה לְגַדְיָא, דְּזַבִּין אַבָּא בִּתְרֵי זוּזֵי...

וְאָתָא מַיָּא וְכָבָה לְנוּרָא, דְּשָׂרַף לְחוּטְרָא,

דְהִכָּה לְכַלְבָּא, דְנָשַׁךְ לְשׁוּנְרָא,
דְאָכְלָה לְגַדְיָא,
דְזַבִּין אַבָּא בִּתְרֵי זוּזֵי...

וְאָתָא תוֹרָא וְשָׁתָה לְמַיָּא, דְכָבָה לְנוּרָא,
דְשָׂרַף לְחוּטְרָא, דְהִכָּה לְכַלְבָּא,
דְנָשַׁךְ לְשׁוּנְרָא, דְאָכְלָה לְגַדְיָא,
דְזַבִּין אַבָּא בִּתְרֵי זוּזֵי...

וְאָתָא הַשׁוֹחֵט וְשָׁחַט לְתוֹרָא, דְשָׁתָה לְמַיָּא
דְכָבָה לְנוּרָא, דְשָׂרַף לְחוּטְרָא,
דְהִכָּה לְכַלְבָּא, דְנָשַׁךְ לְשׁוּנְרָא,
דְאָכְלָה לְגַדְיָא,
דְזַבִּין אַבָּא בִּתְרֵי זוּזֵי...

וְאָתָא מַלְאַךְ הַמָּוֶת וְשָׁחַט לְשׁוֹחֵט,
דְשָׁחַט לְתוֹרָא, דְשָׁתָה לְמַיָּא
דְכָבָה לְנוּרָא, דְשָׂרַף לְחוּטְרָא,
דְהִכָּה לְכַלְבָּא, דְנָשַׁךְ לְשׁוּנְרָא,
דְאָכְלָה לְגַדְיָא,
דְזַבִּין אַבָּא בִּתְרֵי זוּזֵי...

וְאָתָא הַקָּדוֹשׁ בָּרוּךְ הוּא
וְשָׁחַט לְמַלְאַךְ הַמָּוֶת, דְשָׁחַט לְשׁוֹחֵט,
דְשָׁחַט לְתוֹרָא, דְשָׁתָה לְמַיָּא
דְכָבָה לְנוּרָא, דְשָׂרַף לְחוּטְרָא,
דְהִכָּה לְכַלְבָּא, דְנָשַׁךְ לְשׁוּנְרָא,
דְאָכְלָה לְגַדְיָא,
דְזַבִּין אַבָּא בִּתְרֵי זוּזֵי...

Chad gadya, chad gadya. D'zabin abba bitrei zuzei.
Chad gadya, chad gadya.

V'ata shunra, v'achlah l'gadya, d'zabin abba bitrei zuzei.
Chad gadya, chad gadya.

V'ata chalba, v'nashach l'shunra, d'achlah l'gadya, dizabin abba bitrei zuzei. Chad gadya, chad gadya.

V'ata chutra, v'hikah l'chalba, d'nashach l'shunra, d'achlah l'gadya, D'zabin abba bitrei zuzei. Chad gadya, chad gadya.

V'ata nura, v'saraf l'chutra, d'hikah l'chalba, d'nashach l'shunra, D'achlah l'gadya, d'zabin abba bitrei zuzei. Chad gadya, chad gadya.

V'ata maya, v'chavah l'nura, d'saraf l'chutra, d'hikah l'chalba, d'nashach l'shunra, d'achlah l'gadya, d'zabin abba bitrei zuzei. Chad gadya, chad gadya.

V'ata tora, v'shatah l'maya, d'chavah l'nura, d'saraf l'chutra, d'hikah l'chalba, d'nashach l'shunra, d'achlah l'gadya, d'zabin abba bitrei zuzei. Chad gadya, chad gadya.

V'ata ha-shochet, v'shachat l'tora, d'shatah l'maya, d'chavah l'nura, d'saraf l'chutra, d'hikah l'chalba, d'nashach l'shunra, d'achlah l'gadya, d'zabin abba bitrei zuzei. Chad gadya, chad gadya.

V'ata malach ha-mavet, v'shachat l'shochet, d'shachat l'tora, d'shatah l'maya, d'chavah l'nura, d'saraf l'chutra, d'hikah l'chalba, d'nashach l'shunra, d'achlah l'gadya, d'zabin abba bitrei zuzei. Chad gadya, chad gadya.

V'ata Ha-Kadosh Baruch Hu, v'shachat l'malach ha-mavet, d'shachat l'shochet, d'shachat l'tora, d'shatah l'maya, d'chavah l'nura, d'saraf l'chutra, d'hikah l'chalba, d'nashach l'shunra, d'achlah l'gadya, d'zabin abba bitrei zuzei. Chad gadya, chad gadya.

Translation:

One baby goat, one baby goat. And along came the Holy One, Blessed is He, and removed the Angel of Death, that killed the butcher, that slaughtered the ox, that drank the water, that put out the fire, that burnt the rod, that hit the dog, that bit the cat, that ate the baby goat, that father bought for two zuz coins. One baby goat, one baby goat.

KI LO NA'EH, KI LO YA'EH

אַדִּיר בִּמְלוּכָה, בָּחוּר כַּהֲלָכָה, גְּדוּדָיו יֹאמְרוּ לוֹ:
לְךָ וּלְךָ, לְךָ כִּי לְךָ, לְךָ אַף לְךָ, לְךָ יְיָ הַמַּמְלָכָה,
כִּי לוֹ נָאֶה, כִּי לוֹ יָאֶה.

דָּגוּל בִּמְלוּכָה, הָדוּר כַּהֲלָכָה, וָתִיקָיו יֹאמְרוּ לוֹ...
זַכַּאי בִּמְלוּכָה, חָסִין כַּהֲלָכָה, טַפְסְרָיו יֹאמְרוּ לוֹ...
יָחִיד בִּמְלוּכָה, כַּבִּיר כַּהֲלָכָה, לִמּוּדָיו יֹאמְרוּ לוֹ...
מָרוֹם בִּמְלוּכָה, נוֹרָא כַּהֲלָכָה, סְבִיבָיו יֹאמְרוּ לוֹ...
עָנָיו בִּמְלוּכָה, פּוֹדֶה כַּהֲלָכָה, צַדִּיקָיו יֹאמְרוּ לוֹ...
קָדוֹשׁ בִּמְלוּכָה, רַחוּם כַּהֲלָכָה, שִׁנְאַנָּיו יֹאמְרוּ לוֹ...
תַּקִּיף בִּמְלוּכָה, תּוֹמֵךְ כַּהֲלָכָה, תְּמִימָיו יֹאמְרוּ לוֹ...

Adir bimluchah, bachur ka-halachah, g'dudav yomru lo:

Chorus:
>L'cha u-l'cha, l'cha ki l'cha,
>l'cha af l'cha, l'cha Adonai ha-mamlacha,
>Ki lo na'eh, ki lo ya'eh.

Dagul bimluchah, hadur ka-halacha, vatikav yomru lo:

(Chorus)

Zakkai bimluchah, chasin ka-halachah, tafs'rav yomru lo:

(Chorus)

Yachid bimluchah, kabir ka-halachah, limudav yomru lo:

(Chorus)

Marom bimluchah, nora ka-halachah, s'vivav yomru lo:

(Chorus)

Anav bimluchah, podeh ka-halachah, tzaddikav yomru lo:

(Chorus)

Kadosh bimluchah, rachum ka-halachah, shinannav yomru lo:

(Chorus)

Takif bimluchah, tomech ka-halachah, t'mimav yomru lo:

(Chorus)

Translation:

Mighty in royalty, chosen of right, His legions say to Him:

Chorus:
> To You, yes to You,
> To You, surely to You,
> To You, truly to You,
> To You, O Lord, kingship belongs,
> Because for You it is fitting,
> For You it is right.

Distinguished in royalty, glorious of right, His legions…
Pure in royalty, firm of right, His legions…
One in royalty, mighty of right, His legions…
Exalted in royalty, feared of right, His legions…
Humble in royalty, redeemer of right, His legions…
Holy in royalty, merciful of right, His legions…
Almighty in royalty, sustainer of right, His legions…

Echad Mi Yodea?

אֶחָד מִי יוֹדֵעַ? אֶחָד אֲנִי יוֹדֵעַ.
אֶחָד אֱלֹהֵינוּ שֶׁבַּשָּׁמַיִם וּבָאָרֶץ.

שְׁנַיִם מִי יוֹדֵעַ? שְׁנַיִם אֲנִי יוֹדֵעַ.
שְׁנֵי לֻחוֹת הַבְּרִית.
אֶחָד אֱלֹהֵינוּ שֶׁבַּשָּׁמַיִם וּבָאָרֶץ.

שְׁלֹשָׁה מִי יוֹדֵעַ? שְׁלֹשָׁה אֲנִי יוֹדֵעַ.
שְׁלֹשָׁה אָבוֹת. שְׁנֵי לְחוֹת הַבְּרִית...

אַרְבַּע מִי יוֹדֵעַ? אַרְבַּע אֲנִי יוֹדֵעַ.
אַרְבַּע אִמָּהוֹת. שְׁלֹשָׁה אָבוֹת...

חֲמִשָּׁה מִי יוֹדֵעַ? חֲמִשָּׁה אֲנִי יוֹדֵעַ.
חֲמִשָּׁה חֻמְשֵׁי תוֹרָה. אַרְבַּע אִמָּהוֹת...

שִׁשָּׁה מִי יוֹדֵעַ? שִׁשָּׁה אֲנִי יוֹדֵעַ.
שִׁשָּׁה סִדְרֵי מִשְׁנָה. חֲמִשָּׁה חֻמְשֵׁי תוֹרָה...

שִׁבְעָה מִי יוֹדֵעַ? שִׁבְעָה אֲנִי יוֹדֵעַ.
שִׁבְעָה יְמֵי שַׁבַּתָּא. שִׁשָּׁה סִדְרֵי מִשְׁנָה...

שְׁמוֹנָה מִי יוֹדֵעַ? שְׁמוֹנָה אֲנִי יוֹדֵעַ.
שְׁמוֹנָה יְמֵי מִילָה. שִׁבְעָה יְמֵי שַׁבַּתָּא...

תִּשְׁעָה מִי יוֹדֵעַ? תִּשְׁעָה אֲנִי יוֹדֵעַ.
תִּשְׁעָה יַרְחֵי לֵדָה. שְׁמוֹנָה יְמֵי מִילָה...

עֲשָׂרָה מִי יוֹדֵעַ? עֲשָׂרָה אֲנִי יוֹדֵעַ.
עֲשָׂרָה דִבְּרַיָּא. תִּשְׁעָה יַרְחֵי לֵדָה...

אַחַד עָשָׂר מִי יוֹדֵעַ? אַחַד עָשָׂר אֲנִי יוֹדֵעַ.
אַחַד עָשָׂר כּוֹכְבַיָּא. עֲשָׂרָה דִבְּרַיָּא...

שְׁנֵים עָשָׂר מִי יוֹדֵעַ? שְׁנֵים עָשָׂר אֲנִי יוֹדֵעַ.
שְׁנֵים עָשָׂר שִׁבְטַיָּא. אַחַד עָשָׂר כּוֹכְבַיָּא...

שְׁלֹשָׁה עָשָׂר מִי יוֹדֵעַ? שְׁלֹשָׁה עָשָׂר אֲנִי יוֹדֵעַ.
שְׁלֹשָׁה עָשָׂר מִדַּיָּא. שְׁנֵים עָשָׂר שִׁבְטַיָּא...

Leader: Echad mi yodea?

All: Echad, ani yodea.

Echad elohenu she-ba-shamayim u-va'aretz

2. Sh'nayim ani yodea. Sh'nei luchot ha-brit. Echad elohenu she-ba-shamayim u-va'aretz.

3. Sh'loshah ani yodea. Sh'loshah avot. Sh'nei luchot ha-brit. Echad elohenu she-ba-shamayim u-va'aretz.

4. Arba ani yodea. Arba imahot. Sh'loshah avot. Sh'nei luchot ha-brit. Echad elohenu she-ba-shamayim u-va'aretz.

5. Chamishah ani yodea. Chamishah chumshei torah. Arba imahot. Sh'loshah avot. Sh'nei luchot ha-brit. Echad elohenu she-ba-shamayim u-va'aretz.

6. Shishah ani yodea. Shishah sidrei mishnah. Chamishah chumshei torah. Arba imahot. Sh'loshah avot. Sh'nei luchot ha-brit. Echad elohenu she-ba-shamayim u-va'aretz.

7. Shiv'ah ani yodea. Shiv'ah y'mei shabbata. Shishah sidrei mishnah. Chamishah chumshei torah. Arba imahot. Sh'loshah avot. Sh'nei luchot ha-brit. Echad elohenu she-ba-shamayim u-va'aretz.

8. Sh'monah ani yodea. Sh'monah y'mei milah. Shiv'ah y'mei shabbata. Shishah sidrei mishnah. Chamishah chumshei torah.

Arba imahot. Sh'loshah avot. Sh'nei luchot ha-brit. Echad elohenu she-ba-shamayim u-va'aretz.

9. Tish'ah ani yodea. Tish'ah yarchei ledah. Sh'monah y'mei milah. Shiv'ah y'mei shabbata. Shishah sidrei mishnah. Chamishah chumshei torah. Arba imahot. Sh'loshah avot. Sh'nei luchot ha-brit. Echad elohenu she-ba-shamayim u-va'aretz.

10. Asarah ani yodea. Asarah dibraya. Tish'ah yarchei ledah. Sh'monah y'mei milah. Shiv'ah y'mei shabbata. Shishah sidrei mishnah. Chamishah chumshei torah. Arba imahot. Sh'loshah avot. Sh'nei luchot ha-brit. Echad elohenu she-ba-shamayim u-va'aretz.

11. Achad-asar ani yodea. Achad-asar kochvaya. Asarah dibraya. Tish'ah yarchei ledah. Sh'monah y'mei milah. Shiv'ah y'mei shabbata. Shishah sidrei mishnah. Chamishah chumshei torah. Arba imahot. Sh'loshah avot. Sh'nei luchot ha-brit. Echad elohenu she-ba-shamayim u-va'aretz.

12. Sh'neim-asar ani yodea. Sh'neim-asar shivtaya. Achad-asar kochvaya. Asarah dibraya. Tish'ah yarchei ledah. Sh'monah y'mei milah. Shiv'ah y'mei shabbata. Shishah sidrei mishnah. Chamishah chumshei torah. Arba imahot. Sh'loshah avot. Sh'nei luchot ha-brit. Echad elohenu she-ba-shamayim u-va'aretz.

13. Sh'loshah-asar ani yodea. Sh'loshah-asar middaya. Sh'neim-asar shivtaya. Achad-asar kochvaya. Asarah dibraya. Tish'ah yarchei ledah. Sh'monah y'mei milah. Shiv'ah y'mei shabbata. Shishah sidrei mishnah. Chamishah chumshei torah. Arba imahot. Sh'loshah avot. Sh'nei luchot ha-brit. Echad elohenu she-ba-shamayim u-va'aretz.

Translation:

Who knows one? I know one.

One is our God in the heavens and the earth.

Who know two? I know two.

Two are the tablets of the law, one is our God.

Who knows three? I know three.

Three are the fathers, two are the tablets.

Who knows four? I know four.

Four are the mothers.

Who knows five? I know five.

Five are the books of the Torah.

Who knows six? I know six.

Six are the orders of the Mishnah.

Who knows seven? I know seven.

Seven are the days of the Sabbath count.

Who knows eight? I know eight.

Eight are the days of circumcision.

Who knows nine? I know nine.

Nine are the months of pregnancy.

Who knows ten? I know ten.

Ten are the commandments.

Who knows eleven? I know eleven.

Eleven are the stars of Joseph's dream.

Who know twelve? I know twelve.

Twelve are the tribes of Israel

Who knows thirteen? I know thirteen.

Thirteen are the attributes of God.

SUGGESTED RECIPES FOR PASSOVER MEAL

For Jew and Gentile, Passover always means a feast. And you don't have to be Jewish to prepare the special dishes eaten at this time. All you need are some measuring spoons, a few ingredients found in most major supermarkets during the Passover season, and these recipes. Many of the recipes make eight to twelve servings, so be sure to invite a big group. Insist that everyone brings a big appetite. May God inhabit your home as you enjoy and worship Him—the true Atonement, the Paschal Lamb of God.

Compiled in this section are mostly traditional Passover recipes as well as some that are not so traditional. If you do not come from an observant Jewish background, you might not be familiar with rules set down by the rabbis of not mixing milk and meat products (*kashrut*). If you are inviting Jewish friends to your seder who keep to these rules, plan you menu accordingly so as not to unintentionally bring offense.

Most importantly, may you have a blessed and tasty Passover season, until the day when we all sit down together with the Lamb of God Himself at the Marriage Supper of Messiah Jesus.

APPETIZERS

At bubbe's house, the Passover meal always began with at least two or three appetizers. Why two or three? Who knows. If bubbe was asked, she would probably answer, "Such skinny children and what a *shanda* (shame) it would have been if you went home hungry from my house!" Make one, make two, make three or four: no one should go home hungry!

Gefilte Fish

2 pounds whitefish
1½ teaspoons pepper
2 pounds pike
3 eggs
2 pounds carp
¾ cup ice water
4 large onions
½ teaspoon sugar
2 quarts water
3 tablespoons matzah meal
4 teaspoons salt
3 carrots, sliced in ¼" rounds

Fillet fish (or have dealer fillet it for you), reserving head, skin and bones. Combine head, skin and bones with 3 sliced onions, 2 quarts water, 2 teaspoons salt and ¾ teaspoon pepper. Bring to rapid boil, lower heat slightly and keep boiling while preparing fish.

Grind or chop fish and remaining onion finely in a food processor or by hand. Add eggs, ice water, sugar, matzah meal and remaining salt and pepper. Continue processing until very fine. Moisten hands. Shape mixture into slightly flattened loaves approximately 3" long, 2" wide and 1" high. Carefully drop loaves into fish stock. Add carrots, cover loosely and cook over low heat 1½ hours. Remove cover for last ½ hour. Cool fish slightly before removing to platter. Strain stock over fish and arrange cooked carrots around it. Chill. Serve with horseradish (comes in jars). Serves 12.

CHOPPED LIVER

1 pound chicken liver, washed and drained
3 medium onions, chopped
1 clove garlic, mashed
¼ cup vegetable oil
2 eggs, hard-boiled
1 teaspoon salt
black pepper (to taste)

Dry chicken livers on paper towels. Sauté onions and mashed garlic in oil until brown. Remove from pan and add chicken livers. Cook until they lose red color. Reduce heat to low and simmer 10 minutes. Remove from heat. Put all ingredients in food processor or blender (half of mixture at one time) or put through fine blade of a food grinder. Blend to fine paste. Serve in small scoops of lettuce leaves as a first course or as a spread on matzot. Serves about 12 as a spread or 6 as first course servings.

Chicken Soup

4 pounds chicken parts
3¼ quarts water
3 onions, peeled
2 cloves garlic
1 bay leaf
2 chicken bouillon cubes
1¼ tablespoons salt
2 carrots, peeled
1 tablespoon dried parsley
1 teaspoon dried dill

Place chicken parts, onions and water in 8-quart pot. Bring to a boil, lower heat and simmer 2-3 hours, skimming foam off top as necessary. Add remaining ingredients EXCEPT dried dill and parsley. Cover and simmer 1-2 more hours. (If desired, soup can be strained at this point.) Add dill and parsley and cook 15 minutes more. Refrigerate overnight. Skim off fat before reheating next day. Serve with knaidlach (recipe following). Makes approximately 10 servings.

Knaidlach (Matzah Balls)

6 eggs, separated
1 teaspoon salt
⅛ teaspoon pepper
1 cup matzah meal
2 tablespoons chicken fat or margarine, melted

Beat egg whites until stiff. Beat egg yolks in separate bowl until light. Add salt, pepper and melted fat to beaten yolks; fold gently into egg whites. Fold in matzah meal one spoonful at a time. Refrigerate at least one hour. Moisten hands and form batter into walnut-sized balls. Drop into rapidly boiling soup or water. Reduce heat and cook slowly, covered, for 30 minutes. Serves 12.

Fat-free Knaidlach

⅓ cup club soda
½ teaspoon salt
⅔ cup matzah meal
2 eggs, separated
1 tablespoon dried parsley

Combine club soda, salt and ⅓ cup matzah meal; form into a smooth paste and refrigerate for 1 hour. Add egg yolks, remaining matzah meal and parsley. Beat egg whites until stiff (but not dry) and fold into mixture. Chill 2 hours in refrigerator. Form into walnut-sized balls and drop into rapidly boiling water or chicken soup. Reduce heat and cook slowly, covered, for 30 minutes. Makes 24 small knaidlach, enough for 6 servings.

Charoset

- 2 tart apples
- ½ cup walnuts
- ¼ teaspoon cinnamon
- 1 teaspoon honey
- 1 tablespoon sweet Passover wine

Core apples (it is not necessary to peel them). Chop apples and walnuts together in food processor or blender or by hand until finely chopped (the size of grape nuts). Use wooden spoon to stir in cinnamon, honey and wine until well blended. Serves 10-12 people; 1 teaspoon to 1 tablespoon per person on piece of matzah.

Sephardi Style Charoset

- 1 15-ounce box of golden raisins
- 20 ounces of Turkish apricots
- 5 cups finely diced walnuts or almonds
- 1 cup applesauce
- ¼-½ cup honey
- 1-2 teaspoons cinnamon
- 2 tablespoons sweet Passover wine

In food processor, finely chop raisins and apricots (use pulse button to prevent over mixing). Mix in diced nuts and add applesauce, honey, cinnamon and Passover wine. Chill till firm.

Beet Borscht

2 quarts hot water
6 beets with tops
¼ teaspoon salt
1 cup sugar
4 tablespoons lemon juice
1 cup sour cream
4 small boiled potatoes, cold

Wash beets and beet tops well. Peel beets. Slice beets into large saucepan. Add chopped beet tops, then add sugar, salt and lemon juice. Reduce heat and simmer ½ hour or until beets are cooked. Serve hot in bowls with rounded tablespoon of sour cream and a cold, boiled potato. Makes four servings.

THE MAIN COURSE

As your guests and family are finishing their last spoonfuls of soup, it's time to bring on the main course. Here again, you have a choice: lamb, turkey, chicken or perhaps meat tzimmes with carrots and sweet potatoes. During Passover, it's inappropriate to use a bread stuffing or any type of flour or thickening agent. Use a delicious matzah dressing, or when necessary, matzah meal can be used to replace flour or cornstarch in most recipes. But remember, whatever you serve, do it generously and with your biggest "Do it for Momma" smile.

Roast Lamb

Have butcher bone and roll a lamb shoulder or leg-figure on ½ to ¾ pound boned and rolled lamb per person. Use 2 cloves of garlic for every 1 pound of lamb. Cut garlic into thin slices. With the point of a sharp knife, make holes in the fatty part of the lamb. Insert garlic slices into holes. Place meat thermometer in the center of the thickest part of the lamb. Roast at 325° F on a rack in a shallow pan until meat thermometer reaches 175° F (medium done) or 180° F (well done)—about 35-40 minutes per pound. Slice thin.

Carrot and Sweet Potato Tzimmes

4 pounds beef brisket or chuck roast
10 large carrots
10 medium white potatoes
6 medium sweet potatoes
2 teaspoons salt
¼ cup brown sugar
1 medium onion, sliced thin
4 tablespoons matzah meal
4 tablespoons melted chicken fat or margarine
cinnamon

Scrape and cut carrots into 2" long pieces. Peel and cut potatoes into 1" thick rounds. Sear beef with onion over high heat in pot large enough to hold all other ingredients. Turn meat frequently until browned on all sides. Add carrots, potatoes, salt and sugar. Add water to cover and bring to a boil. Reduce flame and cook over low heat for 2½ to 3 hours, until meat is tender enough to pierce with fork. Liquid should be reduced by about half at this point; if it reduces too quickly, add a little more water. Remove onion from pot.

Pour contents into baking pan. Sauté matzah meal in melted fat. Add 3 tablespoons of tzimmes liquid to make a thickening agent. Mix thickening agent evenly throughout the baking pan. Sprinkle a little cinnamon on top and bake at 350° F for 30-40 minutes. Serves at least 12 people.

STUFFINGS FOR ROAST TURKEY OR CHICKEN

Matzah Farfel Stuffing

½ cup ice water
3½ cups matzah farfel or crumbled matzot (matzot should be crumbled into pea-sized bits)
3 eggs
1 teaspoon salt
4 tablespoons margarine or chicken fat, melted
1 onion, finely chopped
1 cup dried prunes, finely chopped
2 tablespoons sugar
pinch cinnamon

Sprinkle matzah farfel or crumbled matzah with ice water. In a large bowl, beat eggs and add the moistened matzah and salt. Sauté chopped onion in melted fat until light brown, and add to matzah mixture. Let cool. Add prunes, cinnamon and sugar. Put mixture back in frying pan and cook over moderate heat, stirring until excess moisture has evaporated. Let cool before stuffing bird in usual manner. Stuffs a 4½ to 5 pound chicken. Recipe can be increased for larger chicken or turkey.

Matzah Stuffing

4 boards matzah
ice water to cover matzot
1 teaspoon salt
3 eggs, beaten
3 tablespoons margarine or chicken fat
1 onion, finely chopped
½ cup celery, finely chopped
1 green pepper, finely chopped

Break matzah into bite-sized pieces. In deep bowl, cover broken matzah with ice water and let stand 5 minutes. Squeeze dry in colander and put in mixing bowl. Add beaten eggs and salt to moist matzah. Melt margarine or chicken fat in pan, and add onion, celery and green pepper. Cook until soft. Add to matzah mixture. Stuffs an average-sized fowl—about a 5 pound chicken. Mixture can be increased to stuff larger chicken or turkey.

Side Dishes

Round out your Passover feast with a variety of side dishes. We have provided a few different kugels here, but also include a green salad and two or three vegetables. Again, the rule here is to make sure no one goes home hungry!

Fruited Cheese and Matzah Kugel

10 boards matzah
3 eggs, beaten
3 cups vanilla yogurt
⅓ cup honey
1 teaspoon cinnamon
½ cup sweetened cranberries
½ cup diced seedless prunes
½ cup diced apricots
½ cup diced dried apple
16 ounces cottage cheese
1 tablespoon butter, melted

Preheat oven to 375° F. Break matzah into small pieces and cover with warm water. Let soften for about 10 minutes. Squeeze out matzah, and drain excess water. Set aside. In large bowl, mix beaten eggs with honey till well combined. Add vanilla yogurt and mix well. Add cottage cheese and cinnamon and mix well. Add dried fruits, then add softened matzah and melted butter and mix thoroughly.

Spray 12 x 9 x 2 inch baking pan with non stick cooking spray. Pour mixture into pan and bake one hour, till kugel is golden brown and a knife inserted into the center comes out clean. Serve warm or cold.

Matzah Meat Kugel

1 pound box of matzah
5 eggs, beaten
2 tablespoons olive oil
1½ teaspoon salt (adjust to taste)
½ teaspoon pepper (adjust to taste)
2 cloves garlic, minced
1 pound onions, chopped
1 pound ground beef

Preheat oven to 350° F. Sauté onion and garlic in oil. Add ground beef and cook till brown. Soften matzah in water, drain well and add softened matzah to meat mixture. Add eggs and seasonings. Spray baking pan with non-stick cooking spray. Pour mixture into pan and bake about 50 minutes, till golden brown.

Matzah Meal Muffins

3 eggs
1 cup water
½ teaspoon salt
1½ cups matzah meal
4 tablespoons margarine or chicken fat
½ teaspoon grated lemon or orange rind

Preheat oven to 350° F. Beat eggs well. Stir in water, salt and matzah meal until batter is thick. Melt margarine or chicken fat and grease muffin pans well. Stir remaining hot fat into batter and blend well. Use 8 large or 16 small muffin cups, filling them two-thirds full. Bake 30 minutes or until lightly browned. Yields 8 large or 16 small muffins.

A FEW EXTRAS

Extras? Was that a groan? Believe me, you'll find these Passover recipes so delicious your family will surprise you with how much they can eat! Included here are recipes for foods that can be eaten at other times during the Passover season—or at any other time during the year. For instance, Matzah Brai, Passover Blintzes and Matzah Pancakes are perfect for breakfast or lunch, served with applesauce or sour cream (except for the meat-filled version of the blintzes). What would bubbe think?

PASSOVER BLINTZES

Blintz wrappers:
8 ounces potato flour
2 eggs
1½ to 2 cups ice water
½ teaspoon salt

Place potato flour in a large bowl. Make a well in the center and break eggs into it. Mix to a thin batter with 1½ cups ice water. Lightly grease a 7" frying pan with oil. Heat greased pan. Pour in sufficient batter to make a thin pancake, tilting pan so entire surface is covered. Cook on one side only until the pancake is set. Flip out of pan, cooked side up, onto sheet of waxed paper. Continue until all batter is used. Put in heaping tablespoon of filling; fold the sides of wrapper; fry in oil until lightly browned on both sides.

Cheese filling:
½ pound dry cottage cheese (or pot cheese)
1 egg
1 tablespoon sugar
1 tablespoon sour cream
⅛ cup butter or margarine, melted
¼ teaspoon salt
½ teaspoon lemon juice

Combine all ingredients and fill blintz wrappers as indicated above.

Meat filling:
1 cup ground beef sautéed with ½ medium onion, minced
OR
1 cup leftover chicken or beef sautéed with ½ medium onion, minced
½ tablespoon chicken fat or margarine, melted
1 egg, beaten
salt and pepper to taste

Combine all ingredients and fill blintz wrappers as indicated above.

Matzah Brai

2 boards matzah
2 eggs
2 tablespoons margarine or butter
salt and pepper to taste

Break matzot into bite-sized pieces. Place broken matzot in colander and run hot water over them until slightly softened. Squeeze matzot dry. Beat eggs, salt and pepper in large bowl. Add drained matzot and mix well. Melt fat in large skillet; add matzot-egg mixture. Cover and cook over moderate heat until lightly browned; turn and brown other side, breaking up matzot with a wooden spoon or spatula. Makes 2 servings.

Matzah Pancakes

½ cup matzah meal
3 tablespoons margarine or butter, melted
1 tablespoon water
3 eggs, beaten
salt and pepper to taste

Combine all ingredients except melted fat and let stand for an hour in refrigerator. Heat fat in large frying pan. Drop mixture by large tablespoonfuls into heated fat and brown well on both sides. Drain on paper towels. Serve with applesauce or sour cream. Makes 10-12 pancakes.

DESSERTS

Who needs dessert? Who doesn't?

There's always room for sweet Passover nut cake, light and almondy macaroons or a generous slice of golden Passover sponge cake. Try your hand at making any of the desserts included here; each is traditional holiday fare.

12 Egg Sponge Cake

12 eggs, separated and at room temperature
2 cups sugar
juice and grated rind of one lemon
¼ cup orange juice
1 cup matzah cake meal
1 cup potato starch
¼ teaspoon salt

Preheat oven to 325° F. Beat egg yolks until thick. Add sugar gradually until mixture is rich and thick. Add lemon juice, rind and orange juice, and continue beating. Sift the matzah cake meal, potato starch and salt together three times. Fold in lightly. Beat egg whites until they form stiff peaks, but stop before they look dry (very important). Gently fold into cake batter. Line bottom of 8 x 14 inch pan with waxed paper or brown paper. Pour in batter and bake for one hour. Invert on cake rake to cool before removing from pan.

Passover Nut Cake

8 eggs, separated and at room temperature
8 tablespoons sugar
½ teaspoon grated lemon rind
1 tablespoon lemon juice
2 tablespoons matzah cake meal
1 cup finely ground almonds or pecans

Preheat oven to 300° F. Beat egg yolks until extremely light and lemon-colored. Add sugar gradually and continue to beat until well blended. Blend in lemon rind, juice, matzah cake meal and ground nuts until well mixed. Beat egg whites until stiff and blend in gently. Pour batter into an ungreased 10-inch spring form pan. Bake for 1 hour or until the cake springs back when pressed lightly in the middle. Invert pan on cake rack to cool. Remove from pan when cool.

Almond Macaroons

5 egg whites
1½ pounds confectioner's sugar
5 tablespoons matzah cake meal
grated rind of one lemon
1 pound blanched almonds, finely ground

Preheat oven to 300° F. Beat egg whites until stiff (but not dry). Add sugar a little at a time until blended in. Fold in matzah cake meal, lemon rind and ground almonds, being careful not to break down egg whites. Drop from a teaspoon onto a foil-lined cookie sheet, leaving one inch between drops. Bake for 15-18 minutes or until lightly browned on top and bottom. Let cool; peel off foil. Makes approximately 3-3½ dozen macaroons.

Easy Coconut Macaroons

1 bag of shredded Baker's sweetened coconut
1 can Eagle Brand sweetened condensed milk
1 12-ounce bag of chocolate chips
1 teaspoon vanilla

Preheat oven to 350°. Mix all ingredients together. Drop onto greased cookie sheet. Bake until toasty; about 10 minutes. Remove from pan. Cool on rack.

Passover Chocolate Cake

¾ cup matzah cake meal, sifted
8 eggs, separated
1½ cups granulated sugar
1 orange—zest and juice
4 tablespoons cocoa
4 tablespoons finely chopped almonds
¼ cup Passover wine

Preheat oven to 350° F. Combine egg yolks and sugar in medium bowl and beat until color is light and mixture is consistency of batter. Add orange zest, orange juice, cocoa, wine, ground nuts and cake meal. Mix well and set aside. In large bowl, beat egg whites until stiff.   Gently fold egg whites into chocolate mixture, one-third at a time. Pour gently into a bundt pan and bake for about 50 minutes. Garnish with sprinkle of powdered sugar and some chocolate curls.

All these recipes have been lovingly prepared, tested and enjoyed in the kitchen of at least one of these Messianic Jewish Bubbes, Mommas and Daughters: Melissa Moskowitz, Phyllis Miller, Janie-sue Wertheim, Hannah Lentz and Laura Wertheim.

PASSOVER RESOURCES

Items for the Passover table:
Many of the ceremonial items on the Passover table can be purchased through the Purple Pomegranate store online at store.jewsforjesus.org. They include a selection of seder plates (metal, ceramic and glass) Passover cups, Elijah cups, *matzah tashes*, *afikoman* bags, candlesticks and much more. Also available is a Passover Kit which includes a pre-set grouping of ceremonial items. Please have a look. For discounts on quantity orders of the *Messianic Family Haggadah*, call 800-366-5521, extension 173.

Other Passover related items that are available from Jews for Jesus include:
Christ in the Passover by Moishe and Ceil Rosen
This fascinating study book by the founder of Jews for Jesus has been expanded and updated and includes new appendices and charts to help you dig deeper into the richness of the holiday and its significance for believers in Y'shua. BK268, 160 pages

Christ in the Passover **DVD or VHS**
David Brickner demonstrates Christ in the Passover before a church audience. Jewish gospel music and beautiful illustrations enhance this engaging program.
Running time: 38 minutes DV035 (DVD), VT035 (VHS)

Walk With Y'shua Through the Jewish Year by Janie-sue Wertheim & Kathy Shapiro
The Jewish holidays (including Y'shua's Birthday and Resurrection) are explained for children ages 8 and up. Beautifully illustrated with suggested activities for each holiday. A fun book for those who love to teach and learn! BK073, 68 pages

Passover e-cards
Send a greeting to friends and family this Passover. A selection of e-cards for Passover are available free at:
jewsforjesus.org/judaica/Passover/e-cards

Craft idea
For those wanting to make their own *matzah tash*, we've provided instructions online at: jewsforjesus.org/passovercraft